Made with ❤ on the BookLeaf Publishing Platform
www.bookleafpub.in
www.bookleafpub.com

Between What Was And What's Next

Poems for a Liminal Journey

Dr. Lori E. Taylor

BookLeaf Publishing

India | USA | UK

Dedication

To those in the in-between;
those wandering and wondering
when and how you'll reach the other side of
the bridge,
the door,
the tunnel,
the wilderness,
the desert

May these poems help you know you're not alone and
give you courage to fully and transparently embrace
transformation.

Preface

Liminal Space is a period of time spent in between what was and what's next. It's a designated season of transition where what you've always known before is no longer in place and you're not sure what's coming to replace it yet. It's the time spent on the threshold of something new.

Here is where transformation can happen, if we let it. There's work to be done in the middle if we don't despise this time and try to rush through it. It's some of the most important inner work we'll do, as we align fully with the Spirit of God and prepare for the next chapter in our story. The postures of our hearts determine the effectiveness of our processing through Liminality.

These poems are organized in groups of three. The first three address the general state of Liminality. The groupings after those initial poems follow the progression of the Six Postures for Thriving In Between: The Posture of a Pilgrim, the Posture of Hospitality, the Posture of Mourning, the Posture of Revision, the Posture of Readiness, and the Posture of Adventure

The following poems are written to help you know you're not alone on the journey. Love walks with you through the darkness, the confusion, the chaos, the questions, and the scary change. God is near. And there's good on the other side.

Acknowledgements

This book of poems would not have been possible without those who encouraged me to pursue a life of holy dissatisfaction.

I thank my parents who nurtured a love of curiosity, inquiry, and learning.

I thank my circle of friends who affirm my love affair with good questions.

I thank my outdoor community, who always challenge me to push higher.

I thank my husband, Chip, and my family, for believing in the value of my words.

1. Taking It Down

Taking down the decorations
A return to what's bare.
Will I like what I find underneath?
Will I have what I need without it?

Naked walls and empty shelves
A fresh canvas waiting to be painted
Who am I in the stripping?
Who will I be through this change?

Between putting off and putting on
Emptiness feels clean, ready for discovery.
What have I lost in the process?
What beckons me to want more?

Only in taking it down
Comes the release of what was, for the embrace of what
could be.

2. Slow Arrivals

Peace arrives slowly, like leaves trading in their green for vibrant colors in Fall, eventually giving way to the quiet dormancy of Winter.

Clarity arrives slowly, like the long walk up a rocky and wooded mountain, offering windowed glimpses along the way of the expansive view to come.

Wisdom arrives slowly, like the tumbled rock on a vast beach, made smooth by relentlessly crashing waves.

Peace leaves quickly when the spirit forgets where the feet are planted.

Clarity leaves quickly when the mind forgets where the eyes are focused.

Wisdom leaves quickly when the body forgets where true strength originates.

Slow down.
Let the arrivals unfold as you
match the slow pace
of the Creator
of Peace,
of Clarity, and
of Wisdom

3. The Origins

When did it begin? The shift
From order to chaos
From form to disarray
From plan to mayhem

Where did it begin? The change
From direction to spinning
From known to unknown
From solid to liquid

How did it begin? The turning
From sure to unsure
From stable to uprooted
From secure to insecure

Why did it begin? The transition
From comfort to discomfort
From settled to unsettled
From control to no control

What did you come from and where are you now?
How and why are you in this place of upheaval?
What if there's something else to it?
What if the truth of the story is not what you think?
What if there's more?

4. The Unexpected Passageways

This passageway is
the unfolding,
the revealing,
the exposing of me.
Each step brings me vulnerably closer to my Creator
And closer to who I have been created to be.

I didn't expect this soul pilgrimage.
I didn't ask for this wandering path.
I didn't want this sifting and testing walk.

But without it I wouldn't embrace
my true worth,
my core self,
my hidden longings.
Each step moves me toward a deeper knowing of Divine
Mystery.
And closer to who I am meant to become.

I'm grateful for this unexpected soul pilgrimage.
I'm grateful for the hiddenness of this wandering path.
I'm grateful for the sifting and testing that has shown me
the Way to walk.

The Way is not a destination.
The Way is a manner of being in the world.
A Way of Faith...Hope...Love

Which I would not have understood
Without walking this painful journey
Through the dark forest of unknowing
Toward healing and wholeness and unspeakable joy

May I forever be open to an unexpected passageway
May my heart forever swell with anticipation at what it
will
unfold
reveal
expose.

May I forever remember that the pilgrimage
will be worth the slow painful movement
Toward more than I could ask or imagine

5. Slow Days

Today is a slow day.
Every step a mile. Every mile a slog.
I can't see where to place my foot next.

Yesterday felt like flying along trails of progress.
Hope blossomed to carpet my path.
I knew where every step should fall.

Today is a low day.
Nothing makes sense.
I just want to sit and be sad and go nowhere.

Yesterday was exciting.
Pathways felt open and free.
I felt the wind at my back and energy surging.

Today is a hard day.
Everything hurts. My blisters are bleeding.
I have no energy for facing this pain.

Yesterday I was strong.

Nothing could derail me. Nothing could deter me.

I thought I was healed. I thought I was free to run.

Today is a slow day.

Today will pass into tomorrow.

Tomorrow might be a yesterday.

Yet I will honor today.

This is the way of the in-between.

I will embrace the slow, low, hard expressions of this
pilgrimage.

I will walk today's miles at today's pace in today's way.

Even if today is a slow day.

6. What If...?

Hurry
Keep up
Don't get behind
You'll be alone
You'll feel ashamed

What if you miss out?

Don't wait
Get it done
Have a plan
You'll look incompetent
You'll seem lazy

What if you waste time?

Control
Take charge
Limit unknowns
You'll feel vulnerable

You'll get lost

What if you appear weak?

Focus
Don't get distracted
Keep moving forward
You'll get derailed
You'll lose time

What if you don't reach your destination?

Rest
Sit in stillness
Let time pass
You'll be refreshed
You'll find your joy again

What if you don't replenish your soul?

Heal
Release your pain
Receive new life
You'll discover freedom
You'll break cycles

What if you could know wholeness?

Appreciate the journey
Don't miss beauty along the way
Take the side trails to the viewpoints
You'll feel present
You'll find true meaningfulness

What if the most important accomplishment is loving
today?

7. Making Room

Making room.
Creating space.
Clearing the clutter, the noise, the buildup of what has
filled up a life.
How can anything new enter
Without first making room?

Where will it sit when every surface is covered?
How can it enter when the door is blocked with what I
already have present?
What do I really need to clear out?

I have so many reasons not to make room.
I've already lost so much. What more do I have to
release?
I like what is there. The clutter is my comfort.
I've worked hard for what is in my space. I deserve to
keep it.
I'm afraid of what I'll find. What if it hurts to see what's
there?

Making room begins with clearing out.
Clearing out begins with seeing what is already in the
room.
Seeing what's in the room begins with facing the
resistance to careful looking.
Facing the resistance to careful looking begins with
courage to move towards it, not turning away from what
is there.
Move toward the burning bush.
Approach with curiosity.
Invite the new voice.
Welcome change.

Hospitality is making room.
It is creating space for what is new.
It begins with clearing out.
It ends with transformation.

8. In the Quiet

What do you hear in the quiet?
Who's voice whispers to you?

Is it the trees telling you to dig your roots deeper?
Is it the wind telling you that you can't always see
what's real?

Are you listening?
Are you stopping and turning your head toward the
silence?

Are the mountains reminding you that the effort is
worth the view?
Are the sunsets reminding you there's beauty in
goodbyes?

What secrets are revealed in breaths?
What truth is exposed in glances?

What is passing by in the noise?

What is missed in distraction?

Give Quiet a chance.
Let Quiet come in and rest in your living room.
Let it put its feet up, offer it some refreshments.
You'll find it makes a gentle houseguest and is very
polite.
It won't stay long but will give you what you need while
it visits.
It will remind you to listen to the revelations of creation,
which speaks without words of its Creator.

9. A Warm Embrace

Between opening of arms and embrace
There is a space

The space is a place of wait
A pause, an abate

To see if what is invited inside
Will respond in kind

Will move toward and not away
As if to say
It will be ok

The pause and wait is scary
My senses wary

But still I will open my arms
Ignore the alarms

Welcoming with love is always worth it.

10. Good Grief

Good grief!
Wait... how is grief possibly good?
When it becomes my teacher
When it reveals what I value most
When it deepens my convictions
When it enlarges my heart
When it raises meaningful questions
When it shows me space for more
When it washes me clean
When it opens me to Love
When it connects me to my people
When it lifts my eyes to God

11. A New Day

A new day is here
but my heart is there
suspended in the instant I lost you

A new day is here
but my thoughts are there
replaying every moment I had you

A new day is here
but my soul is there
clenched in the longing for more of you

A new day is here
but my anger is there
waiting to consume what took you

A new day is here
but I want to be there
living the dreams I still have of you

A new day is here
but how can I be
when here is not where you are
How do I live this new day?

12. Relief

Relief is annoying to pursue
It's always just beyond reach
Not quite fully in my grasp
Slipping through my fingers like water
Leaving evidence that I almost had it.

Relief makes such bold promises,
but it never sticks around
flirting with me just enough to entice
but sneaking out the back door
as soon as I offer my number.

Relief scares me a little
sometimes lurking in shadowed spaces
making me want to find it
even though it sits among monsters
and joining it there would destroy me.

Relief shows up in mysterious places
Often not where I'm looking

strangely joining me when I've given up
taking me by surprise
when I need it most.

It seems to me I usually spot it Lasting Relief holding
hands with Love.

13. Understanding

To open
To expose
To reveal
Unpacking.

To look
To feel
To heal
Unburdening

To ask
To doubt
To detach
Unlearning

To rebuild
To revise
To realign
Understanding

14. My Pack

What I carry is hard to look at
Sometimes it feels too heavy
I wonder if I even need it anymore

But I carry it anyway

It was given to me
And collected by me
And sometimes forced on me

But I carry it anyway

I'm afraid if I look at it
I won't know what to do with it
Some of it I know I like and some I know I don't.

But I carry it anyway.

What happens if I discard what's in there?
Who will I be with an empty pack?

I don't want it to define me anymore.

But I carry it anyway.

Lord give me the courage to sort through this mess.
Give me the wisdom to know what to keep and what to
release.
I give you permission to put in there what you want, not
what I want.

And I'll carry it anyway.

15. The Songwriter

I think I hear a song
It has a slow beat and a subtle rhythm
Sometimes it sounds like a heartbeat, steady

I try to hear the tune
I strain my ears to pick up the melody
Sometimes it sounds like the wind, whispering

I want to know the words
I sing along with what's in my heart
Sometimes it sounds like a prayer, lifting

I'd like to know this song
But it's not mine to create
You're writing this music, expertly.

Will you teach me your song?

16. Simplicity

Simplicity
Complicity with accumulation makes simplicity an
amalgamation
of letting go
of saying No
of bowing low

To lay duplicity at the feet of concentricity
to find the center place
to know what to erase
to create some open space

Identify the toxicity of much and more-ing,
the priority of storing
what we don't need
the monster of greed
we feed

Let simplicity have its chances
To show how it enhances

A life where Love advances
To Thriving

29

17. Wise Counsel

Can you listen to Love when it whispers
through the voice of a wise mentor
saying what you don't want to hear
but what you absolutely need?

Can you listen to Love when it shouts
through the silence of a listening friend
reflecting back to you what your heart knows
but doesn't want to accept?

Can you listen to Love when it sings
through the pages of an ancient Book
serenading you with songs you thought you knew
but resonate differently now?

Can you listen to Love when it speaks
through the counsel of a trusted guide
directing you around dangers you didn't see
but once you do you can avoid them?

Can you listen to Love when it questions
through the innocent voice of a child
zeroing in on the one key Truth
you most needed to remember?

Can you listen to Love's wise counsel?

18. A Celebration of Presence

I will build an altar in this desolate desert
Made of jagged stones, quarried from a layered mind
A lasting reminder of Love present
In the fierce landscape
In the dry valley
In the scorching heat
A Celebration of Presence

I will build an altar in this tangled jungle
Made of vines torn from frayed emotions
A lasting reminder of Love present
In the ripping
In the drenching
In the wrenching
A Celebration of Presence

I will build an altar in this seeded field
Made of clods of packed dirt, dug from a hardened heart
A lasting reminder of Love present

In the tilling
In the waiting
In the reaping
A Celebration of Presence

I will build an altar at the edge of this promised land
A lasting reminder of Love carrying me through the
flooding river
Faithful in the wilderness
Who will be faithful ahead
I will remember
To Celebrate Presence

19. Courage New

Courage looks like a hand held open
Accepting the grasp of someone new

Courage looks like a heart held open
Accepting the feel of a dream new

Courage looks like a plan held open
Accepting the challenge of vision new

Courage looks like a mind held open
Accepting the discomfort of a concept new

Courage looks like arms held open
Accepting the weight of burdens new

Courage looks like a stance held open
Accepting the readiness of a calling new

Courage looks like eyes held open
Accepting the view from a mountaintop new

Courage looks like a soul held open
Accepting the healing of known Love new

20. Minding the Middle

Accepting and anticipating adventure adds awareness of attitudes of antipathy, where avoidance of anxiety-inducing actions acts as a asylum against affliction or adversity

Are you friends with risk?
OR Do you despise and avoid possible loss?

Are you comfortable with discomfort?
OR Do you demand safety and security?

Are you open to new experiences?
OR Do you crave the control of the known?

Are you ready for failure?
OR Do you stick close to what is guaranteed?

Maybe there's meaning in making miniscule movements that matter; minding the middle might mainly mean more meaningful meditative miens.

Give yourself grace in the grey space, actively accepting appeals to adventure but making the most of mini-movements toward meaningful discomfort.

We can't contain courage continuously. We can commit to creatively cultivating change.

21. Curious

Curiosity has it's own reasons for existing, they say.
If you're curious, you find lots of interesting things to do,
they say.
Curiosity is the thirst of the soul, they say.
But curiosity is dangerous.
It killed the cat.

Curiosity is the engine of achievement, they say.
Curiosity is the cure for boredom, they say.
Curiosity is the wick of the candle of learning, they say.
But curiosity is risky.
It fuels insubordination.

Curiosity is invincible in nature, they say.
Curiosity is awakened by good teaching, they say.
Curiosity is what leads us down new paths, they say.
But curiosity is restless.
Once it's satisfied, it quickly finds another lover.

Curiosity fuels the search for truth, they say.

Curiosity dies with age, they say.

Curiosity makes the discovery of possibilities possible,
they say.

But curiosity is in essence, hope.

Once we discover it, it discovers us.